To Chuck Thank you for the supp

Butterfly Flow:
A Book of Poetry

Adrienne Charleston

Love

CONTENTS

ACKNOWLEDGMENTS

I would like to thank my son, Maleek Brown, for all of his love and support and unknowingly pushing me to limits I never knew I could overcome. I love you with all of my heart and soul.

A big thank you to W.E. for putting the fire under me to publish all of the poems I had just sitting around. You convinced me that I was worthy of a book and of greatness. Thank you again.

CATERPILLAR STAGE

Caterpillar: The Feeding Stage – We are feeding our minds and our souls with all that surrounds us. We are experiencing life and taking in all of the information from those experiences.

We delight in the beauty of the butterfly, but rarely admit the changes it has gone through to achieve that beauty – Maya Angelou

Love

How can you tell when you are in love? Most people can tell you when they are not in love. What is the deciding factor? You hear people say "I think I am in Love." Love is a feeling, not a thought process. Like the feeling I get when he smiles at me. The feeling I get when he looks at me. The feeling I get when he talks with me; when he holds my hand. I can't begin to describe the feeling I get from his gentle kiss. Would I say I am in love? I will know in due time.

The Carl Thomas Effect
(The II - dt)

It was love at first sight
I saw him from across the room and it felt right
I watched him and how he moved
Carl sang and I began to groove
After the show was the after party
I got a closer look and I was not sorry
Then there was the way he looked at me
We had a connection, how could this be
We spoke very briefly, it was not long
But the attraction was very, very strong
To not jump on him right then, took all of my might
I made sure he didn't leave my sight
He is not only dark, handsome and tall
He is just like me and that says it all
Our birthdays are the same day
And it is amazing that we feel the same way
The hours I spent with him, I can't explain
There was so much pleasure and so much pain
The pain was in me, because I felt myself falling so fast
The pleasure came being with him as each second passed
His touch, his kisses and his smooth soft skin
I want to be with him again and again
We talk everyday
I can't believe I have so much to say
I want to take it slow
Just to see where this thing goes
Maybe he is the one for what I want to do
Since he is a Gemini, maybe he is the two

Spinning - dh

You have me spinning
And all we've done is talk
You have me spinning
And we took a very short walk
You have me spinning
From the moment you said hello
You have me spinning
I am not sure I want you to know
You have me spinning
I am not sure why
You have me spinning
Like no other guy
You have me spinning
I wanted to kiss you when we first met
You have me spinning
I don't know how much more dizzying this can get
You have me spinning
I am ready to leave today
You have me spinning
Take you to a beach, far, far away
You have me spinning
We haven't even had our first date
You have me spinning
I just know it is going to be great
You have me spinning
I want to see you A.S.A.P.
You have me spinning
I hope you want to see me
Why you may ask
Because you have me spinning

Dream of beautiful things – jt

Dream of beautiful things
Are not the words expected
Dream of beautiful things
Broke through a heart that is very protected
Dream of beautiful things
From a person just met
Dream of beautiful things
No worries of regret
Dream of beautiful things
A first date, things are new
Dream of beautiful things
A date so pure and true
Dream of beautiful things
A kiss so tender and sweet
Dream of beautiful things
Who thought we'd ever meet
Dream of beautiful things
A man wants and desires me
Dream of beautiful things
And also enjoys my company
Dream of beautiful things
Of being held and hugged so tight
Dream of beautiful things
Who thought it would feel so right
Dream of beautiful things
The feelings that stirred from that gentle kiss
Dream of beautiful things
I wonder if my heart can take the risk
Dream of beautiful things
Possibly having someone who cares
Dream of beautiful things
Of Someone who will be there

Dream of beautiful things
The thought alone, shakes me to my soul
Dream of beautiful things
But I don't want to continue to be cold
Dream of beautiful things
Let's see where things go with J
Dream of beautiful things
Maybe he can make my dreams reality

I Look at You - rh

I look at you
And I see what can be
I look at you
And I see you and me
I look at you
And I see my present and my past
I look at you
And I see you as my last
I look at you
And I see us going the distance
I look at you
And I must continue with my persistence
I look at you
And all feels right
I look at you
And I want to hold you all night
I look at you
And I see a strong, confident man
I look at you
And you are more than I can stand
I look at you
And I see forever
I look at you
And wonder what it would be like if we were together
I look at you
And I want you so much
I look at you
And I feel your touch
I look at you
And that's all I want to do
I look at you
And hope you see me too.

Every Time My Phone Rings - ct

Every time my phone rings
I look and hope it's you
Wanting for my phone to ring
To know you are thinking of me too
I want my phone to ring
So I can see your smiling face
Although my phone is a reminder
That you are not in my space
From the time I allowed you to ring my phone
You have made me smile
Soon my phone will lead me to you
Where I can stay a while
I really enjoy your call
And even when you text
At night I must hear your voice
Before I lay to rest
My phone is my gateway
A way for us to be together
Through my phone you open me up
And I want the feeling to last forever
When we talk on the phone
It makes me feel as if you are close by
Even when you text
Just to say Hi
I know our day is coming
And my phone will play an important part
Of how you reached over the miles
And into my heart
So, Every time my phone rings
I look in hopes that it is you
Wanting for my phone to ring
To know you are thinking of me too

Perfect (for me) - ag

You know those lists
The ones some women make
All that they are looking for
In a perfect mate
I may have written one of those
A time or two
The crazy thing is
That it describes you
From your knowledge, to your personality, to your look
To being a nerd and even your name
You match and exceed me in different ways
But, almost as if we were the same
You asked if I believe in love at first sight
And I didn't respond
That's because I believe in love at first touch
And your energy flowed through me like a bomb
You've swept me off my feet
And gently placed me back down
I want to be with you forever
But maybe next time around
You have touched my soul and spirit
Like no other has before
You are my perfect fit
And I want more
I want you in so many ways
I hope one day you will see
We should try each other out
Because you are perfect – for me

Kryptonite - dh

Kryptonite makes you vulnerable
And feel things you would never feel
It has you open to all the forces of the world
It weakens your defenses
Kryptonite - with its beautiful green glow
It looks so bright
Unassuming even
If given to you
You will willingly take it
Embrace it
You are my Kryptonite
You have opened this superwoman up
You make me feel vulnerable
My defenses are down
And beautiful you are
Kryptonite has been introduced to me
Not to hurt
But to improve
To Inquire
To grow
To make this superwoman
A better woman
Kryptonite
Who knew something so unexpected
So different
And so seemingly wrong
Would turn out to be
So wonderful and bright
As the energy it gives off
Kryptonite

Why you

You make me stupid and feel like I can accomplish anything at the same time. You actually make me feel something period. You help me understand that I am wonderful and others can see it. When I am with you, that is all I want............. To be with you.

Should I tell him - dc

I want to tell him I love him
But I don't want to push him away
I want to tell him I love him
And I want to be with him everyday
I want to tell him I love him
Oh, but what would I do
I want to tell him I love him
If he doesn't say I love you too
I want to tell him I love him
But I want things to remain the same
I want to tell him I love him
And I know things will change
I want to tell him I love him

I Want to Talk to You

I want to talk to you
Though you seem so far away
I want to talk to you
Although we talk everyday
I want to talk to you
To let you know my innermost thoughts and fears
I want to talk to you
But I don't want you to see my tears
I want to talk to you
In a way you could understand
I want to talk to you
Just for you to be there for me if you can
I want to talk to you
To help you realize and help you see
I want to talk to you
Hopefully you still like the other side of me
I want to talk to you
And tell you how I feel
I want to talk to you
And hope you know I am real
I want to talk to you
Through all my hurt and my pain
I want to talk to you
I know I have nothing to gain
I want to talk to you
To open up and let you know
I want to talk to you
Maybe one day, we will see how this goes.

Let me count the ways - ct

Sitting on the couch
I have so much to do
But instead of doing work
I find myself thinking of you
You are gone for a little while
I am trying not to count the days
I miss you so much
Let me count the ways
I miss hearing your voice
And your NY accent
I miss being close to you
And smelling your scent
I miss your arms
And the way you wrap me up just so
I miss you making plans
And I just get up and go
I miss all of your kisses
And how you put them all over my face
I miss holding your hand
No matter the time or place
I miss being near you
And feeling your energy
I enjoy our alone time together
When it is just you and me
As I am sitting here counting
I know there are many I have missed
I could go on for hours about you
Not to mention our first kiss
I have a yearning for you
And I want to let it out
When you return
You will see what it is all about

So, as I sit here on the couch
Trying to figure out what to do
The number one thought
Is missing you

The Things I Would do for You – mw

The things I would do for you
And you ain't even know
The things I would do for you
And you didn't even show
The things I would do for you
Is give you all of me
The things I would do for you
And you didn't even see
The things I would do for you
No one would compare
The things I would do for you
And you didn't even care
The things I would do for you
The list could go on and on
The things I would do for you
But alas, you are gone

Mr. Green

Green is my favorite color
And it always makes me smile
So, the very thought of Mr. Green
Stretches my face about a mile
All dressed in Grey
He was smooth, confident and secure
I didn't know what to say
Mr. Green grabbed my hand, spun me around
And we began to dance
His moves were nice and matched mine
I never stood a chance
When the dance was over, Mr. Green left me
Standing there, wanting more
If I only knew what Mr. Green
Had in store
Mr. Green did return to me
To dance and give me a few kisses on my hand
I believe that intelligent Mr. Green
Knew that was all I could stand
The he told me
Why we couldn't be together on this day
I was disappointed because sometimes life,
Just gets in the way
I understood everything he said
Sometimes we have different ties
Mr. Green said, maybe next lifetime
And I thought, maybe we'll be butterflies
So, yeah, green is my favorite color
It reminds me of love, happiness and fun
Now I have more reasons for that color to be around
And Mr. Green is one

Wasted - kh

Wasted is the wine
I purchased for our night together
Wasted is the time
I put into making the perfect night
Wasted is the rose
I had for you that has now wilted away
Wasted are the clothes
I was to wear for you that night
Wasted are the cupcakes
That were oh so sweet
Wasted are the plans I had to break
To spend time with you
Wasted are my feelings
'Cause you can't continue to disappoint me and care
Wasted is my healing
'Cause you won't let me go and I can't let you go

The Breakdown - kh

I keep looking at the phone
But it doesn't ring
I keep looking at the phone
Not one single thing
I haven't heard from you in days
I can only assume you don't care
I am not reaching out to you again
I will not dare
But if you call
I will pick up the phone
For the feelings I have
Are not all gone
I just know now
What I must do
Pull back even more
And not get caught up into you
I will continue to date
And look around
For whatever we had
You caused to breakdown

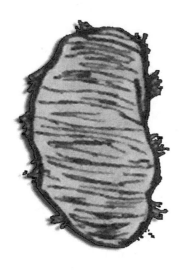

CHRYSALIS STAGE

Chrysalis: The Transition Stage – We are processing all of the information gathered during the caterpillar stage and learning from it.

Meditation is the process of transformation and beautification of soul from a leaf-eating caterpillar to a nectar-sipping butterfly. It grows with the wings of love and compassion – Amit Ray, Meditation: Insights and Inspirations

I Don't Have Time

I have come to the conclusion
That I don't have time for Love
Between therapizing others
Writing poems
Promoting my artists
Performing at shows
Doing events
And even speaking engagements
I have come to the conclusion
That I don't have time for Love
Between taking care of me
Going out dancing
Learning myself
Loving myself
And living my life
I have come to the conclusion
That I don't have time for Love
Between the men who want to change me
The men who want to use me
The men that just want my body
The men that want to control me
And the men that just don't want me
I have come to the conclusion
That I don't have time for Love
No matter how much I am open
No matter how many guys I give a chance
No matter how many dates I have been on
No matter how many ways I try to meet a different type
And no matter how approachable I try to be
I have come to the conclusion
That I don't have time for Love

This conclusion that I have come to
May or may not be true
I think this is a better option than the truth
That Love doesn't have time for me

Down in the dumps

Down in the dumps
Don't know what to do
I want to feel you
But you have left me too
You've left me all alone
With that empty feeling
When you were here
I was full and my mind was reeling
I cherished every moment
But now you're gone
I did everything I could to keep you
But I guess that was wrong
It seems as if life can't go on without you
But I will prevail
And when I have you again
I will not fail
I miss you because you are everything
And there is nothing above
At last I will speak your name
And you will return to me......
Love

The Pain - kh

The pain, the pain, the pain
The pain hurts so deep
The pain, the pain, the pain
The pain of you leaving me
The pain, the pain, the pain
The pain I just can't explain
The pain, the pain, the pain
The pain makes the inside rain
The pain, the pain, the pain
The pain seems as if to never halt
The pain, the pain, the pain
The pain I feel is all you fault
The pain, the pain, the pain
The pain that you stopped calling, Why?
The pain, the pain, the pain
The pain that you didn't have the courage to say good bye
The pain, the pain, the pain
The pain that I am so far away
The pain, the pain, the pain
The pain I can do nothing about on this day
The pain, the pain, the pain
The pain I feel because I told you I love you
The pain, the pain, the pain
The pain I feel because you never said I love you too
The pain, the pain, the pain
The pain of having to start over
The pain, the pain, the pain
The pain of finding another friend and lover

The pain, the pain, the pain
The pain will pass, for I am strong and things will get better
The pain, the pain, the pain
The pain it took me to write this to you, but you will never read
this letter

Adrienne Charleston

I thought you were different - mw

Things didn't work out
But I thought you were different
I felt love beginning to sprout
Because I thought you were different
I crossed the line
Because I thought you were different
I was left behind
Thinking you were different
Maybe I gave too much too soon
Because I thought you were different
Maybe I gave you too much room
Because I thought you were different
Maybe we should have just remained friends
But I thought you were different
Now we are at the end
Because I thought you were different
Trying with you, I do not regret
Because if felt different
The time we spent, I won't forget
Because it felt different
I gave you a piece of my heart
Because I thought you were different
And it has all fallen apart
Because you were not different

We will never be - cw

Even though we have history
We will never be
Even though you say you love me
We will never be
Even though I have feelings for you too
We will never be
Even though I will do anything for you
We will never be
Even though, I can't say no
We will never be
Even though you think it should be so
We will never be
Even though I used to want no other
We will never be
Even if we lived close to one another
We will never be
Even though you will make a good mate
We will never be
Even though the love we make is great
We will never be
Even though we may both really try
We will never be
Even though you have never made me cry
We will never be
Even though you just called me
We will never be
Even though I said I will see
We will never be
Even though we will never be
I am always excited for you to see me

The Helper

Look at me. Oh, you think you don't know who I am, but you do. You see, I am the woman you would call a helper. I help men through hard times. Divorce, lost job, money problems, housing issues, child support or even child custody. Come see me. I am the strong woman who draws weak men or just men with issues. They want me. They need me. They make me feel loved. Loved, wanted, needed; that's everything I could ask for. At least until...................Until he is divorced, has a job, has money, a place to stay or able to see his children. Then I, the helper, am out of the picture. If you didn't hear the first time, the helper is a strong woman. So the helper is good enough to support a man mentally and physically, but too strong to be with him when he can stand on his own two feet. I am too much for a regular man who only thinks he is strong and too much for a strong man because I am still stronger than he. So, for those of you who need me and want me, I am right here. Did you expect anything less? I am the helper, but you can reach me at 1-800-HELP-HIM.

That someone

Have things gone so wrong
So wrong in my life
That all I find a man for
Is to make love oh so right
Have I made the wrong choice?
Are my standards too high?
I want someone to spend my time with
Should I choose just anyone to get by?
I want a man my age
With intelligence and can talk with me
Someone with goals or achievements
Something they are or will soon be
I want a man that is open and honest
Not afraid of me and what I bring
A man that is strong and secure
And okay if I buy him a ring
Someone to hold me tight
When the nights are cold
Someone I enjoy being with at all times
Until the time we are old
Someone who loves me, just the way I am
No questions asked
Someone I can spend my future with
And make a wonderful past
Maybe I'm asking for too much
Should I be happy with what I got
Maybe I'll find him one day
Then again, maybe not
I'll just keep on going
Taking things one day at a time
The man for me is out there
And one day, he'll be mine

Afraid

It is one thing to be desired, but another thing to be loved. I want to be loved. Now, I am just afraid. Not sure if I want to marry again. Not sure if I will get into another serious relationship. I am just afraid. Afraid of being hurt again. Afraid of giving myself and getting nothing in return, again. Afraid of being left with nothing, again. Just, plain, afraid!!

Anticipation

Anxiety and fear
Of laying eyes on you again
Of talking to you face-to-face again
Of you holding me again
Of us kissing again
Of you being inside me again
Of us laying together again
Of the thoughts of us being together
Wanting and waiting
For me to lay eyes on you again
For our conversations to be face-to-face again
For you to hold me again
For us to kiss again
For you to be inside me again
For us to lay side by side again
For us to be together
Anticipation
Of Love

Addict

Call me a heroin addict
I love to get high
But heroin is not my drug of choice
That I use to get by
My drug is one of newness
I am in search of every day
It is one of feeling
With a big price to pay
It is a feeling I've experienced
Once or twice before
But the more I search
A lock is on every door
I am running and running
And I chase to no avail
The feeling of the first high
Keeps coming up as a fail
Yet, I keep searching
For the next time to feel
I keep searching
For it all to become real
I want the feeling to be
Quick, hard and fast
Sometimes I am not even sure
If I care if it will last
Right now, my high is gone
And I am really feenin
All that I am looking to obtain
I am not sure of the meaning
But the high that I am in search of
The one drug I crave
Is the true love of a man
A high that I would not trade

I don't have a dealer
To provide what I need
I have gone cold turkey
And no way to proceed
Yes, I am an addict
My drug I do miss
I admit to my addiction
And still in search for my next fix

Possibilities - db

Possibilities are endless
Is how the saying goes
Possibilities are questionable
Because no one really knows
Possibilities have the possibility
Of coming true
Possibilities of what could occur
If I open up to you
Possibilities can be frightening
Because the future you cannot see
Possibilities are always there
Of you hurting me
Possibilities can be positive
Everything could work out great
Possibilities may be the best thing
You could be my perfect mate
Possibilities are always there
That you can break my wall down
Possibilities that once it is gone
You may not want to be around
Possibilities that you may
Actually like what you receive
Possibilities that we are together
And without you I can't breath
Possibilities that it all goes wrong
And we cannot recover
Possibilities that at some point
You may not want to be my lover
Possibilities that time goes by
And we do not miss a day
Possibilities that you say let's go
And I just say okay

Possibilities of getting lost
Lost in love
Possibilities that you were sent to me
Sent from above
Possibilities that I will get over
My fear and let you be my second rose
Possibilities are endless
Is how the saying goes

HATE - gw

I hate that you know me
And can see right to my soul
I hate you know my heart
Even though I want it to be cold
I hate I think about you
And you tell me you think about me
I hate I want to be with you
And you just can't see
I hate I don't really hate you
When you have disappointed me so
I hate I can't see you when I want
And I can't let you go
I hate I get excited to hear from you
With even the slightest text or call
I hate after being so strong
You are the one to make me fall
I hate I've never told you
How I really feel
I hate I'm not sure how you would take things
Or know that I am being real
I hate that these feelings scare me
And I don't know what to do
I hate that even more than that
I am scared of you

When Can I See You Again - mw

When can I see you again
Is the song that comes to mind
We have spent one night together
And I am ready for the next time
It has taken years
To cross that line
Now I am ready to stay
And I am not looking behind
I hate that I waited
So long to let you know
We will have to wait and see
Where this all goes
Your energy is strong
And I can't deny
That it matches with mine
Without the first try
I am at ease and calm
Just lying next to you
It can be overwhelming
I am not sure what to do
I am going to feel these feelings
That you have made emerge
I am going to see what happens
I know I have the courage
So, if you are up for it
To see what this all brings
Maybe we can find our
Very own song to sing

Priorities kh v. ct

I remember when he told me
That I was not a priority
I cried and cried and was very upset
Because he meant so much to me
We continued to talk from time to time
And see each other here and there
But deep down, I already knew the outcome
That this was not going anywhere
When he made the revelation that he could not find anyone better
And all the love he had he wanted to share
All I could think was that the priority list hasn't changed
And I am not sure how much I care
Time has gone by
And our communication has been cut off altogether
I am happy about that
And I don't have to speak to him forever
Then you come along sometime later
With all of your happiness and joy
You bring out the best in me
Like I am a little girl and you a little boy
These feelings are so new to me
And I want to fight them with all I have
But you keep pushing right through
And it sometimes makes me so mad
It has not been that long
Since you and I have started on this journey
But you let me know from the very beginning
That I will be one of your priorities
I am not sure if you understand
How all of this has made me feel
It makes me want to open up to you
To be me and to be real

You see, you have already shown me
What it feels like to be around a real man
So, I'd like to thank you for being you
And taking me the way I am

Love songs

Were all of those love songs right
About when you are in love
You can't sleep at night
Your thought are consumed
With memories of the last moments together
Your thought are consumed
With being with him forever
Every love song reminds
You of his smile
Even though you saw him last week
It seems as if it has been a while
You've gotten rid of the others
Without him asking
You talk more about your feelings
Without masking
I guess those love songs are true
Because love makes you crazy
Counting the days, minutes and hours
Until your next encounter can make you hazy
Sitting at work thinking of him
So all you are doing is muddling
Wishing you were home
With him on the couch cuddling
Thinking about his touch, his kiss
And being wrapped up in his arms
And knowing when you are there
You are safe from harm
Yes, those love songs have it right
And in love is where I be
I think the best part about it
Is knowing he loves me

Thank you - jc

Out of all the men
That have seen me cry
You didn't tell me to stop
Or even ask why
You took my tears
And wiped them with you hand
You held me close
To show me you understand
You didn't try to convince me
That things will be okay
You allowed me to have the moment
With no words to say
You came to me at a time
When I was upset and distraught
Your kind of understanding
Cannot be taught
So, I thank you for being you
That is all I can ask anyone to be
And for taking your time
To be there for me

BUTTERFLY STAGE

Butterfly: Adult stage – We take all that we have learned back into the world, as we are new, whole, and loving ourselves.

What the caterpillar calls the end of the world, the master calls a butterfly – Richard Bach

Butterfly in the Wind

You see me
You want me
You say you love my energy and my free spirit
But once I let you in
The lassos come out
You are trying to put a saddle on the back of this butterfly
To control where she goes and what she does
You say you love the glow that I have
But you want to replace it with a light bulb that only you control
the switch
You like my energy
But you want to put it in a jar on a shelf for only you to sip from
when needed
Don't you know you can't bottle the wind
You have to go with the flow
If it blows too hard, button up your coat and hold on
As for me, I am free like the wind
Or better yet a butterfly in the wind
Going where the wind takes me
The only way to be with me is to allow me to be free
Allow me to be me
If I am happy with myself and my endeavors
I am happy with the person that supports me and all of my flights
If you are secure in who you are
And you can provide a secure homing area for this butterfly to land
and rest
Who knows, maybe you will be able to go on a couple of wind
rides with me

Adrienne Charleston

Damsel in this dress

Most men want a damsel in distress
When they meet me
They see a damsel in a dress
I don't need to be saved
I'm financially stable
I will not ask for money
I have a couple of jobs
So, my time is just as important as his
I am able to do things on my own
I will not sit around waiting for a man to contact me
I have options
Even if I choose to be alone
I will not chase a man
I do not need anything of a material manner
But I do want things
I want a man to listen to me
And understand what I have to say
To want me for who I am
I want a man to love me inside and out
I want a man to treat me like a lady
And make me feel like a woman
But, I say again
Most men want a damsel in distress
But, I am just a damsel in a dress
A damsel in this dress

Force! – dh

You force me to let go
You force me to be free
You force me to relax
You force me to be me
You force me to be open
And break down my wall
You force me to share
And give it my all
You force me to learn
More than I ever knew
You force me to be okay
With what I want to do
You force me to look inside
And understand my feelings
You force me to give myself to you
And now my head is spinning
You force me to go deep
And actually feel my emotions
You force me to know that they go deeper
More like an ocean
So, with all of that said
And what you've forced me to do
No matter what happens
It will remain true
You force me to let go
You force me to be free
You force me to relax
You force me to be me

Adrienne Charleston

This man – mm

What is there to be afraid of?
He is just a man.
Maybe because men have hurt you in the past. Not physically, but that may have been easier to bear and hide than the emotional scars that have left you wounded.
You may be stronger, happier, even better than you were before.
But, out of fear, you are these things with yourself, for yourself and by yourself.
How can you allow a man into this sanctuary you have built for yourself?
Are you afraid he may tear apart all that you have built for yourself, for your mental stability?
This man is already on his way. He has to get past the booby traps and snipers you have around your heart.
This man is moving in silence and with confidence.
Yes, he is a man, but he is not that man.
At this point, he is not the man that hurt you, mistreated you, did not want you and just did not love you the way you deserve to be loved.
No, this man, this man may be different.
This man is already different in your eyes, heart, mind, body and soul.
Not that this man is the be all to end all, but this man deserves you.
All of you. Not the bits and pieces you give to others.
He deserves to get to know the real you.
You deserve to allow it to happen.
Get to know this man.
Find out if he is what you want.
So, I ask you again, What are you afraid of?
After all, he is just a man.

I Love You - ct

I Love you
If I don't tell you today
I Love you
If I don't tell you tomorrow
I Love you
If I am not able to talk to you
I Love you
If I am not able to see you
I Love you
When our time together is short
I Love you
When we are together for days
I Love you
When we are upset with each other
I Love you
When everything is going great
I Love you
When I hear your voice in the morning
I Love you
When I receive a text from you
I Love you
When I think of you
I Love you
When I am working
I Love you
I may not always say it
Just know, trust and believe
That I Love you

Adrienne Charleston

The Man - gw

Long gone is the shy boy
I had the biggest crush on
Long gone is the shy boy
Performing Bobby Brown songs
Long gone is the shy boy
Who didn't move too fast
Long gone is the shy boy
That most girls looked past
Long gone is the shy boy
So meek and mild
Long gone is the shy boy
Far from being wild
Long gone is the shy boy
Who took his time to mature
Now stands the man
Taking control of his future
Now stands the man
So confident and strong
Now stands the man
Who slow dances to Bobby Brown songs
Now stands the man
Who is exciting and loves to have fun
Now stands the man
Who is a self proclaimed "Wild One"
Now stands the man
Who knows how to make a woman feel cared for
Now stands the man
Who gives massages and opens doors
Now stands the man
For whom my feelings still grow
Now stands the man
I want to continue to get to know

The High – mw

Coming down off the high
That is you
You do things to me
And I don't know what I am going through
You scare me with the feelings
The ones you have created
I am so high,
I may have to be sedated
Just being around you
Is where I want to be
You provide what I have been looking for
Sacred Simplicity
The talking is minimal,
But I feel the connection
My heart has been dead
And you are the resurrection
Your touch and your kiss
Are like no other
When I am near you I want more kisses
Give me another and another
I enjoy being close to you
You make my temperature rise
I enjoy lying with you
And looking into your eyes
Your smile makes my heart skip
And I sometimes have to catch my breath
I am not sure where this is going
But I am willing to take the steps
Maybe I should have said something sooner
Who knows what time has been wasted
But we can't go back now
And the sweetness has been tasted

Just know that every time I see you
I have to calm myself down
Because the high that is you
Keeps me flying around

Love Jones

When I came home today, it just happened to be on. Love Jones. The most realistic love story I have ever seen. "I am dancing a bright beam of light. I am remembering love." These were the last two lines of the poem that brought Nina and Darius back together. The way they fell in love; the things they went through. It showed the biggest thing to mess up a relationship is trust. This small word is more important than the word "love" because you can love someone, but if you can't trust them, you can't be with them. I used to be a very trusting person and it has come back to hurt me most every time. At a point, I stopped trusting.............. even myself. Now, I believe I will not find what I am looking for unless I trust others.

Alone on Valentine's Day

I am in this room, alone, trying to feel sorry for myself, but for the first time in a long time it isn't working. I am finally happy with me. The love of my life called me at 6:30 this morning and he made my day (my son). I am happy not worrying about pleasing others or what others think. I am not saying I'm perfect. I would like to lose about 5 pounds. I would like my hair a different color, then I will be good to go. But whether or not I lose 5 pounds or get my hair the perfect color I will continue to be happy. There are good days and bad days, but as long as I have joy within, I will be happy forever.

A Real Man

I am looking for someone like my father. I am looking for a man that is hard working, allows me to be me and loves and takes care of me. I am looking for someone like my son, laid back, easy going and not crowding or needy. I am looking for someone like my brother, a strong man, makes me feel safe and I know things will be taken care of. I am looking for someone like my best friend, open, honest, crazy, loves to have fun, spontaneous, take care of his woman, family and friends. I am looking for a man that is not unlike any other man in my life. My definition of a real man.

I am a Contradiction

I am the good girl men want to wife
I am the bad girl men want as their mistress
I am the sweet girl women want to befriend
I am the diva women want to be
I am the free spirit most wish they had
I am the confidence that intimidates most
I am the boss that gets things done
I am the worker who is part of the team
I am the daughter that takes care of the family
I am the mother that guides her child
I am the soldier that is able to lead
I am the civilian living the life
I am the conservative one that others turn to
I am the wild child that others want to hang with
I am the one who has it all together
I am the one falling apart
I am the one with all of the knowledge
I am the one who is naïve
I am the strong outspoken woman
I am the weak shy girl
I am the tomboy that's cool with the fellas
I am the woman of today
I am all of the above and then some
I am a walking contradiction

Me, Myself and I

I wake up with the same 3 people I went to bed with:
Me, Myself and I
They will never waiver, falter, cheat nor lie
These are the most important 3 people in my life
They don't cause me pain, stress or strife
It may sound selfish, but they will never leave my side
When I say let's go, they are always ready to ride
They may not always agree, so at times I am torn
But I love them all, because together we were born
Because there are 3, a tie is easily broken
We come together, with no words spoken
They help, guide and set us on our way
I am blessed to have these consultants each and every day
The relationship we have together will always last
We hang out often and we always have a blast
There is no one out there like them, no one can duplicate
I really like each and every one of them, they are all great
They know my deepest secrets and all I've been through
When things are going on, they are the first ones I run to
They are happy right along with me, when I am down they pick me
up
When I am unmotivated to do something, they give me a swift kick
in the butt
Again, I love them all for I am they, and you know who they be
They are me, myself and I, the 1 that is 3

Me and Her

The person you see
Is not all there is to me
There is a person inside
The person I hide
She is more real and more raw
She is someone you never saw
At first meeting you are drawn to the happy one
She's great, beautiful and lots of fun
You fall for her from the jump
Because she is all you want
Then there is the other person
When she comes out, they go and run
She is open emotional and true
But the truth is not what others run to
This person wants the same as most
For someone to be with her and not get ghost
She wants to be hugged loved and respected
Not punished for the unexpected
She wants to be out and about with the others
Not hiding and running for cover
She is not a person that is bad
Just someone that was treated as such,
So, at times, she is sad
The thing is we are called by one name
Because we are one in the same
Understanding her is understanding me
But no one wants to know how that will be
So, she has me and I have her
With no one else will we be together

Happy

Sometimes I find that I am happy
For no real reason
Sometimes I find that I am happy
Just because it's my season
Sometimes I find that I am happy
To reach many goals in my life
Sometimes I find that I am happy
Because of all my struggle and strife
Sometimes I find that I am happy
Because I can be myself
Sometimes I find that I am happy
So, I put my troubles on the shelf
Sometimes I find that I am happy
Just because it is a new day
Sometimes I find that I am happy
And I want to dance and play
Sometimes I find that I am happy
So, I smile at everyone I see
Sometimes I find that I am happy
About the woman I've grown to be

Adrienne Charleston

Sometimes............Love

Sometimes I am the best
Sometimes I am tired
Sometimes I wish
Sometimes I hope
Sometimes I am the Best
Best at seeing others through their stuff
Best at taking care of others
Best at taking care of me
Best at making myself a priority
Sometimes I am tired
Tired of being strong
Tired of taking care of others
Tired of being without a companion
Tired of being an option
Sometimes I wish
Wish to do more for others
Wish for more money
Wish to lie on the beach, in the sun
Wish for more time to myself
Sometimes I hope
Hope for my perfect companion
Hope for understanding
Hope for that "All I need" kind of love
Hope for someone to "Rub me on my back and say baby it'll be
okay"
And Sometimes, Just Sometimes
I am the best at Love
I am tire of Love
I wish for Love
I hope for Love

Butterfly Flow

You can't tame a butterfly
You have to let her be
For she has crawled around for way too long
And the world she must see
There was a period of time she was locked away
In a shell all her own
Now she is able to fly
And the world she must roam
For as you know
Her time here will not last forever
So, cherish the time you have
And the times you are together
You see, the wind dictates her direction
And where she will go
If you are to travel with the butterfly
Then just follow her flow

ABOUT THE AUTHOR

Adrienne Charleston decided at the age of 25 that she wanted to help people reach their full potential. At that time, she found herself 7 years into the military as a Legal Specialist and some years left on her obligation. So, she made a plan. This plan took years to come to fruition, but she never gave up and kept moving forward despite the speedbumps life placed in her way. Adrienne completed that active duty obligation and then some. She then joined the Army Reserve as a Mental Health Specialist. While in the Reserves, she was working toward Military Retirement and on her degrees. Adrienne went back to her home town and attended Fayetteville State University. She graduated with honors with a BS is Psychology and a minor in Criminal Justice. Adrienne then attended North Carolina Central University where she received her Master's in Psychology. She retired from the military before graduating with her Master's. Adrienne then tested and became a Licensed Psychological Associate and began practicing Psychology in the state of North Carolina.

Adrienne has been writing poetry for about 15 years as an outlet. She was encouraged by a friend to publish her work and participate in spoken word events. Adrienne has since been inspired to write more books with the Butterfly Flow mantra. You can find more information about release dates, merchandise and event dates on all of her social media sites under the name: Adrienne Charleston; and on her website: www.adrienne-charleston.com

All art work provided by: www.higherupsuniversity.com

Made in the USA
Middletown, DE
29 May 2016